50

Broccoli

Recipes!

Dedicated to my family.

Introduction

50 Delicious broccoli recipes!

We could all use a little more broccoli in our diet! Broccoli is in the category of superfoods. It is loaded with fiber, antioxidants to fight cancer and vitamin C to aid in iron absorption.

Broccoli is low in calories, fat free and contains no cholesterol.

Eating more vegetables like broccoli gives you more energy and helps you lose weight!

Certain nutrients in broccoli helps the skin detoxify itself, so it helps reduce the risk of skin cancer caused by over exposure to UV rays.

Nutrients in broccoli also help reduce the risk and slow the growth of breast cancer, cervical cancer and prostate cancer.

Broccoli can help fight osteoarthritis because the vitamin K, calcium and other nutrients in broccoli help strengthen your bones.

Soluble fibers in broccoli helps reduce cholesterol, aids in digestion and controls over eating, making broccoli the ideal ingredients for those trying to lose weight.

The potassium and magnesium in broccoli helps to regulate blood pressure.

With this cookbook, I have given you 50 great ways to enjoy broccoli with a list of tasty, mouth-watering recipes so it is easy to enjoy your veggies!

Perfect to take to a party or a pot-luck at work.

This recipe book includes 50 broccoli recipes for you to make for dinner, family meals, barbecues, pool parties or get-togethers. Enjoy!

Broccoli Coleslaw

Ingredients:

1 cup olive oil
1/3 cup distilled white vinegar
1/2 cup white sugar
1 (3 oz.) package chicken flavored ramen noodles, crushed, seasoning packet reserved
1 large head fresh broccoli, diced
2 carrots, grated
2 bunches green onions, chopped
1 cup sunflower seeds

Directions:

1. In a small bowl combine oil, vinegar, sugar and the seasoning packet from the ramen noodles.
2. Mix well and refrigerate at least one hour before serving, or overnight.
3. In a large bowl combine broccoli, carrots, green onions and sunflower seeds.
4. Crush ramen noodles and stir in.
5. Pour dressing over salad about 10 minutes before serving.
6. Serve and enjoy!

Broccoli Salad

Ingredients:

1/2 pound bacon
2 heads fresh broccoli, chopped
1 bunch green onions, chopped
1/2 cup shredded carrots salt and pepper to taste
1 cup mayonnaise
1/2 cup distilled white vinegar
1/2 cup raisins (optional)

Directions:

1. Place bacon in a large, deep skillet.
2. Cook over medium high heat until evenly brown.
3. Drain, crumble and set aside.
4. In a large bowl, combine the bacon, broccoli, green onions, carrots and salt and pepper.
5. In a small bowl whisk together the mayonnaise and vinegar.
6. Pour dressing over vegetables and toss to coat evenly.
7. Chill for 1 hour before serving.
8. Serve and enjoy!

Broccoli and Mushroom Salad

Ingredients:

4 slices bacon
4 cups broccoli florets
1/4 red onion, finely chopped
1/4 cup raisins
1 cup chopped cremini mushrooms
1/4 cup sunflower seed kernels
1 cup mayonnaise
1/4 cup white sugar
3 tbsps. apple cider vinegar salt and ground black pepper to taste

Directions:

1. Place bacon in a large, deep skillet, and cook over medium-high heat, turning occasionally, until evenly browned, about 10 minutes.
2. Drain bacon slices on a paper towel-lined plate; crumble bacon.
3. Combine broccoli, red onion, raisins, mushrooms, sunflower seeds, and crumbled bacon in a large bowl.
4. Mix mayonnaise, sugar, vinegar, salt, and black pepper in a bowl until well blended.
5. Pour mayonnaise mixture over vegetables; toss to coat.
6. Serve and enjoy!

Broccoli Raisin Salad

Ingredients:

1 pound bacon
6 cups chopped broccoli
1 small red onion, finely chopped
1 cup raisins
1 cup mayonnaise
1/2 cup white sugar 2 tbsps. white vinegar
1 (3 oz.) package sunflower seeds

Directions:

1. Place bacon in a large skillet and cook over medium-high heat, turning occasionally, until evenly browned, about 10 minutes.
2. Drain the bacon slices on paper towels and cool. Chop bacon.
3. Mix broccoli, bacon, red onion, and raisins in a bowl.
4. Whisk mayonnaise, sugar, and vinegar together in a bowl; stir dressing into broccoli mixture until evenly coated.
5. Cover bowl and refrigerate for flavors to blend, about 1 hour.
6. Sprinkle with sunflower seeds.
7. Serve and enjoy!

Broccoli and Grape Salad

Ingredients:

8 slices bacon
1/3 cup sunflower seed kernels
1 large head broccoli, cut into bite-size pieces
1/3 cup diced red onion
1 cup seedless red grapes, halved 1 cup mayonnaise
3 tbsps. apple cider vinegar
2 tbsps. white sugar ground black pepper to taste

Directions:

1. Place bacon in a large skillet and cook over medium-high heat, turning occasionally, until evenly browned, about 10 minutes. Drain bacon slices on paper towels. Crumble 7 slices of bacon; mix with sunflower seeds in a resealable bag.
2. Combine broccoli, onion, and grapes in a bowl.
3. Crumble the remaining bacon slice. Whisk mayonnaise, vinegar, sugar, and black pepper together in a bowl; fold in the 1 slice crumbled bacon. Pour dressing over broccoli mixture; toss to coat evenly. Cover bowl with plastic wrap and refrigerate for flavors to blend, about 2 hours.
4. Sprinkle bacon-sunflower seed mixture over salad before serving; mix well.
5. Serve and enjoy!

Broccoli Cranberry Salad

Ingredients:

6 strips bacon
1 cup mayonnaise
1/4 cup white sugar
2 tbsps. red wine vinegar
3 heads broccoli, finely chopped
1/2 cup chopped red onion
1/3 cup salted sunflower kernels, toasted
1/4 cup dried cranberries

Directions:

1. Place the bacon in a large skillet and cook over medium-high heat, turning occasionally, until evenly browned, about 10 minutes.
2. Drain bacon slices on paper towels and crumble.
3. Whisk mayonnaise, vinegar, and sugar in a bowl; refrigerate until ready to combine with salad.
4. Combine broccoli, onion, bacon, sunflower seeds, and cranberries in a large bowl.
5. Drizzle mayonnaise dressing over broccoli mixture; toss to coat.
6. Serve and enjoy!

Broccoli Curry

Ingredients:

1 large head broccoli, cut into florets
1/2 red bell pepper, chopped
1/2 cup dried cranberries
1/2 cup chopped walnuts
4 scallions, chopped
3/4 cup mayonnaise
2 tbsps. fresh lime juice
2 tbsps. apple cider vinegar
1 tbsp. white sugar
1 tbsp. curry powder, or more to taste
1/2 tsp. cayenne pepper

Directions:

1. Mix broccoli, red bell pepper, cranberries, walnuts, and scallions together in a large bowl.
2. Whisk mayonnaise, lime juice, vinegar, sugar, curry powder, and cayenne pepper together in a bowl until smooth; pour over broccoli mixture and toss to coat. Refrigerate salad until flavors blend, 2 hours to overnight. Toss well before serving.
3. Serve and enjoy!

Broccoli Strawberry Salad

Ingredients:

8 cups fresh broccoli florets
2 cups fresh strawberries, quartered
1 (8 oz.) pkg. Colby-Monterey Jack cheese, cut into ½" cubes
1 cup mayonnaise
2 tbsps. white sugar
1 tsp. cider vinegar
1/4 cup sliced almonds, toasted

Directions:

1. Combine broccoli, strawberries, and Colby-Monterey Jack cheese in a large bowl.
2. Whisk mayonnaise, sugar, and vinegar together in another bowl until blended; pour over broccoli mixture.
3. Sprinkle almonds over broccoli salad and gently toss to coat.
4. Cover with plastic wrap and refrigerate until chilled, 1 to 2 hours.
5. Serve and enjoy!

Broccoli and Ramen Noodle Salad

Ingredients:

1 (16 oz.) package broccoli coleslaw mix
2 (3 oz.) packages chicken flavored ramen noodles
1 bunch green onions, chopped 1 cup unsalted peanuts
1 cup sunflower seeds 1/2 cup white sugar 1/4 cup vegetable oil
1/3 cup cider vinegar

Directions:

1. In a large salad bowl, combine the slaw, broken noodles and green onions.
2. Whisk together the sugar, oil, vinegar and ramen seasoning packets.
3. Pour over salad and toss to evenly coat.
4. Refrigerate until chilled; top with peanuts and sunflower seeds before serving.
5. Serve and enjoy!

Broccoli and Tortellini Salad

Ingredients:

6 slices bacon
20 oz. cheese-filled tortellini
1/2 cup mayonnaise
1/2 cup white sugar
2 tsps. cider vinegar
3 heads fresh broccoli, cut into florets
1 cup raisins
1 cup sunflower seeds
1 red onion, finely chopped

Directions:

1. Place bacon in a large, deep skillet. Cook over medium high heat until evenly brown. Drain, crumble and set aside.
2. Bring a large pot of lightly salted water to a boil. Cook tortellini in boiling water for 8 to 10 minutes or until al dente. Drain, and rinse under cold water.
3. In a small bowl, mix together mayonnaise, sugar and vinegar to make the dressing.
4. In a large bowl, combine broccoli, tortellini, bacon, raisins, sunflower seeds and red onion. Pour dressing over salad, and toss.
5. Serve and enjoy!

Sesame Broccoli

Ingredients:

1 tbsp. sesame oil
2 cups chopped broccoli 1 tbsp. sesame seeds
1 green bell pepper, sliced

Directions:

1. Heat oil in a large skillet over medium-high heat.
2. Sauté broccoli and sesame seeds for 2 minutes.
3. Stir in bell pepper and cook 2 to 3 minutes, until pepper is tender crisp.
4. Serve and enjoy!

Cream of Broccoli Soup

Ingredients:

1 head fresh broccoli
3 tbsps. butter
3 tbsps. minced onion
1 stalk celery with leaves, chopped
3 tbsps. all-purpose flour
1 cup milk
1 cup heavy cream
2 cubes chicken bouillon
1 tsp. Worcestershire sauce
2 pinches paprika
1 tsp. salt
1 cup shredded mozzarella cheese

Directions:

1. Place broccoli in a medium saucepan with water to cover, bring to a boil, then reduce heat and simmer until tender, 15 minutes.
2. Remove broccoli and reserve cooking water.
3. In the same pan, melt butter over medium heat.
4. Cook onions and celery in butter until tender, 10 to 15 minutes.
5. Stir in flour, milk and cream. Dissolve bouillon in 2 cups reserved broccoli water. Stir into soup. Season with Worcestershire, paprika and salt.
6. Stir in cheese and cook 10 minutes more.
7. Serve and enjoy!

Cheese of Broccoli Soup

Ingredients:

1 (10 oz.) package frozen chopped broccoli
1 (10.75 oz.) can condensed cream of mushroom soup
1 1/4 cups milk
Milk
8 oz. processed cheese
Salt and pepper to taste

Directions:

1. Prepare broccoli according to directions. Drain off excess water.
2. Add cream of mushroom soup and one can of milk to broccoli.
3. Stir and heat thoroughly on low.
4. Add cheese, stirring until melted. Add salt and pepper to taste.
5. Your quick and creamy soup is ready to serve!
6. Serve and enjoy!

Fried Broccoli Bites

Ingredients:

3 tbsps. Dijon mustard
4 tbsps. honey
2 cups broccoli florets
1 cup shredded Cheddar cheese
1 egg 1 cup milk
1/2 cup sifted all-purpose flour
1/2 tsp. baking powder
1/2 tsp. salt
1/2 tsp. vegetable oil
1/2 cup vegetable oil for frying

Directions:

1. To make the sauce: In a small bowl, stir together the mustard and honey. Set aside.
2. Chop florets into small pieces or pulse lightly in food processor. Toss in a mixing bowl with shredded cheese.
3. Set aside.
4. Beat egg and stir in the milk. Sift flour, baking powder, and salt together and combine them with the egg and milk mixture, beating well. Beat in 1/2 tsp. oil as well. Pour mixture over broccoli and cheese and toss to coat well.
5. In a large skillet or saucepan heat oil until hot.
6. Drop broccoli mixture by spoonfuls into oil and fry until golden brown.
7. Serve with honey mustard sauce.
8. Serve and enjoy!

Broccoli and Cauliflower Gratin

Ingredients:

2 tsps. butter
2 heads cauliflower 2 heads broccoli
1/2 cup butter 1/2 cup all-purpose flour
4 cups milk 1 tbsp. mustard powder
1 tbsp. Worcestershire sauce
1/2 tsp. ground black pepper
2 cups grated Cheddar cheese
1 cup Italian seasoned bread crumbs
1/4 cup extra-virgin olive oil 1 pinch paprika, or to taste

Directions:

1. Preheat oven to 375 degrees F (190 degrees C).
2. Grease a baking dish with 2 tsps. butter.
3. Core and cut cauliflower into large florets.
4. Cut broccoli into large florets; peel and quarter broccoli stalks.
5. Bring a large stockpot of water to a boil; add cauliflower and boil until tender but still firm, 8 to 10 minutes. Transfer cauliflower to strainer using a slotted spoon; run under cold water to stop cooking. Add broccoli stalks to stockpot and boil 3 minutes; add broccoli florets to stockpot and boil until stalks and florets are tender but still firm, about 5 minutes more. Transfer broccoli to strainer and run under cold water to stop cooking. Dry cauliflower and broccoli with paper towels and place in prepared baking dish.
6. Melt 1/2 cup butter in saucepan over medium heat. Whisk in flour to form a thick paste.
7. Continue whisking constantly until flour begins to brown, about 4 minutes. Add milk and bring to a boil, whisking constantly, until sauce thickens, 2 to 4 minutes more. Remove sauce from heat; whisk in mustard, Worcestershire sauce, and pepper. Whisk in Cheddar cheese until melted and fully incorporated.
8. Pour cheese sauce over cauliflower and broccoli.
9. Mix bread crumbs and olive oil together in a small bowl.
10. Top vegetable and sauce mixture with bread crumb mixture.
11. Sprinkle paprika over bread crumb mixture.
12. Bake in preheated oven until bubbly and golden brown, about 30 minutes.
13. Serve and enjoy!

Broccoli Mac and Cheese

Ingredients:

1 (16 oz.) package elbow macaroni
2 tsps. butter
1 head broccoli, cut into florets
1 small onion, chopped
3 eggs
2 cups milk salt and pepper to taste
1/4 tsp. adobo seasoning
2 cups shredded Cheddar cheese, divided
2 cups shredded mozzarella cheese, divided
20 frozen tater tots

Directions:

1. Cook macaroni according to package directions.
2. Drain.
3. Preheat an oven to 350 degrees F (175 degrees C).
4. Grease a 9x13 inch baking dish.
5. Cook the bacon in a skillet until crisp.
6. Drain the bacon slices on paper towels.
7. Crumble the bacon and set aside.
8. Heat 1 tsp. of butter in a skillet over medium heat.
9. Stir in the broccoli and onion; cook and stir until the onion has softened and turned translucent, about 5 minutes.
10. Whisk together the eggs, the remaining 1 tsp. of butter, and milk in a large bowl.
11. Season with salt, pepper, and adobo seasoning.
12. Stir in 1 cup of Cheddar cheese, 1 cup of mozzarella cheese, the broccoli mixture and half of the tater tots.
13. Place macaroni into the baking dish and pour the cheese mixture over the pasta, mixing well.
14. Top with the remaining Cheddar and mozzarella cheese, bacon, and tater tots.
15. Cover with aluminum foil.
16. Bake until golden brown, about 40 to 45 minutes.
17. Serve and enjoy!

Broccoli Pie

Ingredients:

2 (10 oz.) packages chopped frozen broccoli, thawed
1/2 cup diced onion
2 cups shredded Cheddar cheese
1/2 cup baking mix 1 egg
1 cup milk salt and pepper to taste

Directions:

1. Preheat oven to 350 degrees F (175 degrees C).
2. Grease a 2 quart casserole dish.
3. Combine broccoli, onions and cheese in prepared dish.
4. In a small bowl whisk together baking mix, egg, milk, salt and pepper.
5. Pour over broccoli mixture.
6. Bake in preheated oven for 35 minutes, or until lightly browned.
7. Serve and enjoy!

Broccoli Soufflé

Ingredients:

1 (14 oz.) bag frozen chopped broccoli, thawed
1/4 cup margarine
1/4 cup all-purpose flour 1 cup milk
3 eggs, beaten
2/3 cup mayonnaise
3 tbsps. chopped onion
salt and ground black pepper to taste
1/2 cup shredded Cheddar cheese

Directions:

1. Preheat oven to 350 degrees F (175 degrees C).
2. Place a steamer insert into a saucepan and fill with water to just below the bottom of the steamer. Bring water to a boil. Add broccoli, cover, and steam until tender, 2 to 4 minutes.
3. Melt margarine in a saucepan over medium heat.
4. Add flour and stir until mixed.
5. Slowly add the milk, stirring to prevent lumps.
6. Cook until white sauce is thickened, about 10 minutes.
7. Combine broccoli, eggs, mayonnaise, and onion in a baking dish; cover with white sauce and stir to combine.
8. Bake in preheated oven for 30 minutes.
9. Sprinkle Cheddar cheese on top and bake until set, about 15 minutes more.
10. Serve and enjoy!

Broccoli Kugel

Ingredients:

1 tbsp. vegetable oil
1 onion, sliced
4 eggs
1 cup mayonnaise
3 tbsps. all-purpose flour
Salt and pepper to taste
2 (16 oz.) bags frozen chopped broccoli, thawed

Directions:

1. Preheat an oven to 375 degrees F (190 degrees C).
2. Grease an 8x8-inch baking dish.
3. Heat the vegetable oil in a skillet over medium heat.
4. Stir in the onion; cook and stir until the onion has softened and turned translucent, about 5 minutes.
5. Reduce heat to medium-low, and continue cooking and stirring until the onion is very tender and dark brown, 15 to 20 minutes more. Set aside.
6. Beat eggs with mayonnaise, flour, salt, and pepper in a large bowl.
7. Stir in broccoli and onion.
8. Pour into the prepared baking dish.
9. Bake in the preheated oven until broccoli is tender, about 90 minutes.
10. Serve and enjoy!

Broccoli and Rice

Ingredients:

1 1/2 cups uncooked long-grain rice
1 tbsp. vegetable oil
1 (16 oz.) package frozen broccoli florets, thawed
3 green onions, diced
2 eggs, beaten
2 tbsps. soy sauce
1/2 tsp. salt
1/4 tsp. ground black pepper

Directions:

1. In a saucepan, bring
2. 3 cups water to a boil. Stir in rice. Reduce heat, cover, and simmer for 20 minutes.
3. Heat oil in a large skillet over medium heat. Sauté broccoli until tender crisp, and add scallions.
4. Remove from skillet.
5. Scramble eggs; return broccoli mixture to pan. Stir in cooked rice, soy sauce, salt and pepper.
6. Serve and enjoy!

Beef with Broccoli Stir Fry

Ingredients:

1/3 cup oyster sauce
2 tsps. sesame oil
1/3 cup sherry
1 tsp. soy sauce
1 tsp. white sugar
1 tsp. cornstarch
3/4 pound beef round steak, cut into 1/8" thick strips
3 tbsps. vegetable oil, plus more if needed
1 thin slice of fresh ginger root
1 clove garlic, peeled and smashed
1 pound broccoli, cut into florets

Directions:

1. Whisk together the oyster sauce, sesame oil, sherry, soy sauce, sugar, and cornstarch in a bowl, and stir until the sugar has dissolved.
2. Place the steak pieces into a shallow bowl, pour the oyster sauce mixture over the meat, stir to coat well, and marinate for at least 30 minutes in refrigerator.
3. Heat vegetable oil in a wok or large skillet over medium-high heat, and stir in the ginger and garlic.
4. Let them sizzle in the hot oil for about 1 minute to flavor the oil, then remove and discard.
5. Stir in the broccoli, and toss and stir in the hot oil until bright green and almost tender, 5 to 7 minutes.
6. Remove the broccoli from the wok, and set aside.
7. Pour a little more oil into the wok, if needed, and stir and toss the beef with the marinade until the sauce forms a glaze on the beef, and the meat is no longer pink, about 5 minutes.
8. Return the cooked broccoli to the wok, and stir until the meat and broccoli are heated through, about 3 minutes.
9. Serve and enjoy!

Broccoli and Rice Stir Fry

Ingredients:

1 1/2 cups uncooked long-grain rice
1 tbsp. vegetable oil
1 (16 oz.) package frozen broccoli florets, thawed
3 green onions, diced
2 eggs, beaten
2 tbsps. soy sauce
1/2 tsp. salt
1/4 tsp. ground black pepper

Directions:

1. In a saucepan, bring 3 cups water to a boil.
2. Stir in rice.
3. Reduce heat, cover, and simmer for 20 minutes.
4. Heat oil in a large skillet over medium heat.
5. Sauté broccoli until tender crisp, and add scallions.
6. Remove from skillet.
7. Scramble eggs; return broccoli mixture to pan. Stir in cooked rice, soy sauce, salt and pepper.
8. Serve and enjoy!

Broccoli Chicken

Ingredients:

1 tbsp. vegetable oil
4 skinless, boneless chicken breast halves
1/2 cup milk
1 (10.75 oz.) can condensed cream of broccoli soup
1 cup shredded Cheddar cheese salt and pepper to taste

Directions:

1. Heat oil in a large skillet over medium heat.
2. Fry chicken breasts until cooked through, about 15 to 20 minutes.
3. Combine the milk and cream of broccoli soup; pour over the chicken. Reduce heat to simmer and cook for a few more minutes.
4. Stir in Cheddar cheese until well blended, and remove from heat. Serve immediately over rice or noodles.
5. Serve and enjoy!

Broccoli Pecan Chicken

Ingredients:

2 tbsps. fresh lemon juice
3/4 cup butter
2 cloves garlic, crushed
1/4 tsp. dried basil
1 tsp. chopped pimento
1 cup chopped pecans
1 1/2 cups chopped fresh broccoli florets
1 small onion, minced
1/2 cup sour cream
1 (3 oz.) package cream cheese
8 skinless, boneless chicken breast halves
1 egg, beaten
1 cup dry bread crumbs
1/2 cup chopped pecans
1 tbsp. vegetable oil

Directions:

1. To Make Broccoli/Cream Cheese Filling:
2. In a medium saucepan over low heat, heat the lemon juice, butter, garlic, basil and pimento until butter or margarine has melted.
3. Add the pecans, broccoli and onion and cook until broccoli is tender.
4. Add the sour cream and cream cheese and mix all together until smooth.
5. Let cool, cover and refrigerate to chill for 30 minutes.
6. Place 1 to 2 tbsps. of the broccoli/cream cheese filling in the center of each chicken breast, roll up, tuck in sides and fasten with toothpicks.
7. Put the egg beat in a shallow dish or bowl, and mix the bread crumbs and 1/2 cup pecans together in another shallow dish or bowl.
8. Dip the chicken rolls in the egg, then in the pecan mixture.
9. Preheat oven to 350 degrees F (175 degrees C).
10. Heat oil in a large skillet over medium high heat and sauté coated chicken rolls in skillet until well browned on both sides, about 2 to 4 minutes each side.
11. Place browned rolls in a lightly greased 9x13 inch baking dish.
12. Bake at 350 degrees F (175 degrees C) for 30 minutes, or until chicken is cooked through and chicken meat is white.
13. Serve with a small portion of leftover broccoli/cream cheese mixture on top of each chicken breast.
14. Serve and enjoy!

Broccoli Pesto

Ingredients:

2 cups chopped broccoli floret
2 cups chopped fresh basil
1/4 cup extra-virgin olive oil
1/4 cup shaved Parmesan cheese
1/4 cup pine nuts
6 cloves garlic, peeled
2 tbsps. vegetable broth, or more if needed
1 pinch cayenne pepper salt and ground black pepper to taste

Directions:

1. Place a steamer insert into a saucepan and fill with water to just below the bottom of the steamer. Bring water to a boil.
2. Add broccoli, cover, and steam until tender, 3 to 5 minutes.
3. Blend steamed broccoli, basil, olive oil,
4. Parmesan cheese, pine nuts, garlic, vegetable broth, cayenne pepper, salt, and black pepper in a blender until smooth and pourable.
5. Serve and enjoy!

Curried Broccoli Couscous

Ingredients:

2 tbsps. olive oil
1/4 bunch broccoli, finely chopped (1 ½ cups)
1 tsp. curry powder
1 cup canned chickpeas, rinsed
1/3 cup golden raisins
Kosher salt
3/4 cup couscous

Directions:

1. In a large saucepan, heat the oil over medium-high heat.
2. Add the broccoli and cook, tossing occasionally, until tender, 2 to 3 minutes.
3. Add the curry powder and stir to combine.
4. Stir in the chickpeas, raisins, 1 cup water, and ½ tsp. salt and bring to a boil.
5. Stir in the couscous, cover, and remove from heat.
6. Let steam 5 minutes, then fluff with a fork.
7. Serve and enjoy!

Broccoli Mashed Potatoes

Ingredients:

1/2 bunch broccoli, finely chopped (3 cups)
1pound Yukon gold potatoes, peeled and cut into ½-inch pieces
1/4cup sour cream
4tbsps. unsalted butter, softened
Kosher salt and black pepper

Directions:

1. Fill a large saucepan with 1 inch of water and fit with a steamer basket.
2. Bring the water to a boil.
3. Place the broccoli and potatoes in the basket, cover, and steam until very tender, 10 to 12 minutes.
4. Drain the vegetables well and return them to the pot.
5. Add the sour cream, butter, ½ tsp. salt, and ¼ tsp. pepper and mash to desired consistency.
6. Serve and enjoy!

Broccoli and Apple Slaw

Ingredients:

1/2cup plain low-fat yogurt
1/4cup mayonnaise
1tablespoon cider vinegar
1 small shallot, finely chopped
Kosher salt and black pepper
1/2 bunch broccoli, finely chopped (3 cups)
1/2 apple, finely chopped
1/4cup dried cranberries
2tbsps. toasted pine nuts

Directions:

1. In a large bowl, stir together the yogurt, mayonnaise, vinegar, shallot, ¾ tsp. salt, and ½ tsp. pepper. Add the broccoli, apple, cranberries, and pine nuts and toss to combine.
2. Serve and enjoy!

Parmesan Roasted Broccoli

Ingredients:

6 cups broccoli florets
1 small red onion, cut into wedges
2 tbsps. olive oil
1/2 cup grated Parmesan
Kosher salt and black pepper

Directions:

3. Heat oven to 425 degrees F.
4. On a rimmed baking sheet, toss the broccoli and onion with the oil and Parmesan and season with ½ tsp. each salt and pepper. Roast, tossing once, until tender, 20 to 25 minutes.
5. Serve and enjoy!

Broccoli Stuffing

Ingredients:

2 (16 oz.) packages frozen chopped broccoli
1 cup shredded Cheddar cheese
2 eggs, beaten 1 onion, minced
1 (10.75 oz.) can condensed cream of mushroom soup
1/2 cup mayonnaise
10 oz. dry bread stuffing mix
1/2 cup butter, melted

Directions:

1. Preheat oven to 350 degrees F (175 degrees C). Cook broccoli according to package instructions. Lightly grease a large baking dish.
2. In a bowl, mix the cheese, eggs, onion, cream of mushroom soup, and mayonnaise.
3. Arrange the cooked broccoli in the prepared baking dish. Pour cheese sauce over broccoli. Spread stuffing mix over the sauce. Drizzle butter over all.
4. Bake 30 minutes in the preheated oven, until bubbly and lightly browned.
5. Serve and enjoy!

Broccoli Cheddar Quiche

Ingredients:

1 ready-to-use refrigerated pie crust (1/2 of 15-oz. pkg.)
1-1/2 cups KRAFT Shredded Cheddar Cheese
1 pkg. (10 oz.) frozen chopped broccoli, thawed, drained
4 eggs
1-1/2 cups half-and-half

Directions:

1. Preheat oven to 375°F. Prepare pie crust as directed on package for unfilled 1-crust pie using 9-inch pie plate.
2. Sprinkle half of the cheese evenly onto bottom of crust.
3. Top with broccoli and remaining cheese.
4. Beat eggs and half-and-half with wire whisk until well blended; pour over ingredients in crust.
5. Bake 40 to 45 min. or until knife inserted in center comes out clean. Let stand 10 min. before serving.
6. Serve and enjoy!

Broccoli Quinoa

Ingredients:

2 cups chopped broccoli
1 3/4 cups vegetable broth
1 cup quinoa
1 cup shredded Cheddar cheese
Salt and ground black pepper to taste

Directions:

1. Combine broccoli, broth, and quinoa in a saucepan; bring to a boil. Reduce heat to medium-low, place a cover on the saucepan, and cook at a simmer until the broth has been absorbed and the quinoa is tender, 15 to 20 minutes.
2. Stir Cheddar cheese into the quinoa, replace the lid, and set aside until the cheese melts, 2 to 3 minutes; season with salt and pepper.
3. Serve and enjoy!

Broccoli Marinara

Ingredients:

2 tbsps. olive oil
1 (14.5 oz.) can diced tomatoes with balsamic vinegar, basil and olive oil
1 pound broccoli florets
2 cloves garlic, chopped salt and pepper to taste

Directions:

1. Heat olive oil in a large skillet over medium heat.
2. Add garlic, and cook for a few minutes, stirring constantly.
3. Pour in the tomatoes with their juices, and simmer until the liquid has reduced by about 1/2. Place the broccoli on top of the tomatoes, and season with a little salt and pepper.
4. Cover, and simmer over low heat for 10 minutes, or until the broccoli is tender.
5. Do not over cook the broccoli, it should be a vibrant green.
6. Pour into a serving dish, and toss to blend with the sauce before serving.
7. Serve and enjoy!

Broccoli and Sausage

Ingredients:

1 pound spicy Italian sausage
1/2 cup olive oil 4 cloves garlic, minced
1 (16 oz.) pkg. cavatelli pasta
1 (16 oz.) pkg. frozen broccoli
1/2 tsp. crushed red pepper flakes
1/4 cup grated Parmesan cheese

Directions:

1. In a skillet, fry sausage over medium heat until no longer pink; drain, and reserve.
2. In the same skillet, cook garlic in olive oil until golden.
3. Meanwhile, bring a large pot of lightly salted water to a boil.
4. Cook pasta in boiling water for 8 to 10 minutes or until done; drain. Three minutes before the end of the cooking time, add broccoli; drain with pasta.
5. In a large serving bowl, toss together the sausage, olive oil and garlic, cavatelli and broccoli, and Parmesan.
6. Season with red pepper flakes.
7. Serve and enjoy!

Indian Broccoli Curry

Ingredients:

4 tbsps. ghee
2 medium onions, chopped
1 tsp. chili powder
1 1/2 tsps. black pepper
2 tsps. cumin
1 tsp. ground coriander
2 tsps. turmeric
1 cup red lentil
1 lemon, juice of
3 cups chicken broth
2 medium broccoli, chopped
1/2 cup dried coconut
1 tbsp. flour
1 tsp. salt
1 cup cashews, coarsely chopped

Directions:

1. Heat butter in saucepan and sauté onions until well browned.
2. Add chili powder, pepper, cumin, coriander and turmeric.
3. Stir and cook, 1 minute.
4. Add lentils, lemon juice, broth and coconut if using.
5. Bring to boil, reduce heat and simmer for 45-55 minutes (if mixture is too thick, you may need to add a little hot water).
6. Steam broccoli for 7 minutes.
7. Plunge broccoli in cold water and set aside.
8. Remove 1/3 cup of liquid from the lentil mixture.
9. Add to flour to form a smooth paste.
10. Return to pan; add broccoli, salt and nuts if using.
11. Simmer for 5 minutes.
12. Serve over Basmati rice.
13. Serve and enjoy!

Mediterranean Roasted Broccoli

Ingredients:

4 cups broccoli florets
1 cup grape tomatoes
1 tbsp. extra-virgin olive oil
2 cloves garlic, minced
1/4 tsp. salt
1/2 tsp. freshly grated lemon zest
1 tbsp. lemon juice
10 pitted black olives, sliced
1 tsp. dried oregano
2 tsps. capers, rinsed

Directions:

1. Preheat oven to 450 degrees F.
2. Toss broccoli, tomatoes, oil, garlic and salt in a large bowl until evenly coated. Spread in an even layer on a baking sheet.
3. Bake until the broccoli begins to brown, 10 to 13 minutes.
4. Meanwhile, combine lemon zest and juice, olives, oregano and capers (if using) in a large bowl.
5. Add the roasted vegetables; stir to combine. Serve warm.
6. Serve and enjoy!

Ginger Broccoli

Ingredients:

1 tbsp. canola oil
2 tbsps. minced garlic
4 tsps. minced fresh ginger
6 cups broccoli florets, trimmed and chopped
3 tbsps. water
1 tbsp. fish sauce
1 tbsp. rice vinegar

Directions:

1. Heat oil in a large skillet over medium-high heat. Add garlic and ginger and cook until fragrant but not browned, 30 seconds to 1 minute. Add broccoli and cook, stirring, until the broccoli is bright green, 2 minutes. Drizzle water and fish sauce over the broccoli; reduce heat to medium, cover and cook until the broccoli is just tender, about 3 minutes.
2. Stir in vinegar just before serving.
3. Serve and enjoy!

Chipotle Orange Broccoli

Ingredients:

1 14-oz. package extra-firm water-packed tofu
1/2 tsp. salt, divided
3 tbsps. canola oil, divided
6 cups broccoli florets
1 cup orange juice
1 tbsp. minced chipotle in adobo
1/2 cup chopped fresh cilantro

Directions:

4. Drain tofu and pat dry; cut into 1/2- to 3/4-inch cubes.
5. Sprinkle tofu on all sides with 1/4 tsp. salt.
6. Heat 2 tbsps. oil in a large nonstick skillet over medium-high heat.
7. Add tofu and cook in a single layer, stirring every couple of minutes, until golden brown, 7 to 9 minutes total.
8. Transfer to a plate.
9. Add the remaining 1 tbsp. oil and broccoli to the pan and sprinkle with the remaining 1/4 tsp. salt; cook, stirring, until the broccoli is bright green, about 1 minute. Add orange juice and chipotle and cook, stirring frequently, until the broccoli is just tender, 2 to 3 minutes more.
10. Return the tofu to the pan. Cook, gently stirring, until the tofu is heated through, 1 to 2 minutes. Remove from the heat and stir in cilantro.
11. Serve and enjoy!

Broccoli Kung Pao Tofu

Ingredients:

1 14-oz. package extra-firm water-packed tofu, rinsed
1/2 tsp. five-spice powder, divided
1 tbsp. canola oil
1/2 cup water
3 tbsps. oyster sauce
1/2 tsp. cornstarch
4 cups broccoli florets trimmed and cut into bite-size pieces
1 yellow bell pepper, cut into 1/2-inch dice
1 tbsp. minced fresh ginger
1 tbsp. minced garlic
2 tbsps. unsalted roasted peanuts
2 tsps. sesame oil

Directions:

1. Pat tofu dry and cut into 1/2-inch cubes.
2. Combine with 1/4 tsp. five-spice powder in a medium bowl.
3. Heat canola oil in a large nonstick skillet over medium-high heat. Add tofu and cook, stirring every 1 to 2 minutes, until golden brown, 7 to 9 minutes total. Transfer to a plate.
4. Meanwhile, whisk water, oyster sauce, cornstarch and the remaining 1/4 tsp. five-spice powder in a small bowl.
5. Add broccoli, yellow and red bell pepper to the pan and cook, stirring occasionally, until beginning to soften, about 4 minutes.
6. Add ginger and garlic and cook, stirring, until fragrant, about 30 seconds. Reduce heat to low, add the oyster sauce mixture and cook, stirring, until thickened, about 30 seconds.
7. Return the tofu to the pan along with peanuts and stir to coat with sauce; stir in hot sesame oil (if using).
8. Serve and enjoy!

Broccoli Ham and Cheese Quiche

Ingredients:

16 oz. frozen hash browns (thawed)
8 eggs, beaten, divided
2 tbsps. all-purpose flour
1 tbsp. canola oil or extra-virgin olive oil
1/4 tsp. salt
2 cups finely chopped broccoli florets
1 cup shredded extra-sharp Cheddar cheese
3/4 cup finely diced smoked ham
3/4 cup reduced-fat sour cream
1/4 cup minced fresh chives
1/8 tsp. freshly ground pepper

Directions:

1. Preheat oven to 375 degrees F.
2. Coat a 9-inch springform pan with cooking spray.
3. Line a rimmed baking sheet with foil.
4. Toss hash browns with 1/4 cup beaten eggs, flour, oil and salt in a medium bowl.
5. Pat the mixture into the bottom and 2 inches up the sides of the prepared springform pan.
6. Bake until the potatoes are beginning to brown at the edges, 35 to 40 minutes.
7. Fill the crust with broccoli, cheese and ham.
8. Whisk the remaining 11/2 cups eggs, sour cream, chives and pepper in a medium bowl.
9. Place the pan on the prepared baking sheet and pour the egg mixture over the filling.
10. Bake the quiche until the center is just set, 50 minutes to 1 hour.
11. Let cool for 15 minutes.
12. Run a knife around the edges to loosen the sides, remove the pan sides and cut the quiche into wedges.
13. Serve and enjoy!

Shrimp with Broccoli

Ingredients:

2/3 cup bottled clam juice, or chicken broth
1 tsp. cornstarch
1 tbsp. minced garlic, divided
3 tsps. extra-virgin olive oil, divided
1/4-1/2 tsp. crushed red pepper
1 lb. raw shrimp, peeled and deveined
1/4 tsp. salt, divided
4 cups broccoli florets
2/3 cup water
2 tbsps. chopped fresh basil, or parsley
1 tsp. lemon juice
Freshly ground pepper, to taste
Lemon wedges

1. ## Directions:

2. Combine clam juice (or broth), cornstarch and half the garlic in a small bowl.
3. Whisk until smooth.
4. Set aside.
5. Heat 1 1/2 tsps. oil in a large nonstick skillet over medium-high heat. Add the remaining garlic and crushed red pepper to taste; cook, stirring, until fragrant but not browned, about 30 seconds. Add shrimp and 1/8 tsp. salt.
6. Sauté until the shrimp are pink, about 3 minutes.
7. Transfer to a bowl.
8. Add the remaining 1 1/2 tsps. oil to the pan.
9. Add broccoli and the remaining 1/8 tsp. salt; cook, stirring, for 1 minute. Add water, cover and cook until the broccoli is crisp-tender, about 3 minutes.
10. Transfer to the bowl with the shrimp.
11. Add the reserved clam juice mixture to the pan and cook, stirring, over medium-high heat, until thickened, 3 to 4 minutes. Stir in basil (or parsley) and season with lemon juice and pepper. Add the shrimp and broccoli; heat through. Serve immediately, with lemon wedges.
12. Serve and enjoy!

Broccoli Lasagne

Ingredients:

9 lasagna noodles
3 tbsps. butter
1 small onion, chopped
2 cloves garlic, chopped
2 tbsps. all-purpose flour
1/4 tsp. ground white pepper
1 tsp. salt, divided
1/8 tsp. ground nutmeg
2 1/2 cups milk
2 tbsps. chopped fresh parsley
1 (15 oz.) container ricotta cheese
1 (10 oz.) package chopped frozen broccoli, thawed and drained
1/4 cup grated Parmesan cheese
2 cups shredded mozzarella cheese, divided

Directions:

1. Preheat oven to 350 degrees F (175 degrees C).
2. Bring a large pot of lightly salted water to a boil.
3. Add pasta and cook for 8 to 10 minutes or until al dente; drain.
4. In a medium saucepan over medium heat, melt butter.
5. Cook onion and garlic in butter until tender. Stir in flour, pepper, 1/2 tsp. salt and nutmeg. Stirring continuously, pour in milk, a little at a time, allowing mixture to thicken. Bring to a boil for 1 minute, then remove from heat and stir in parsley. Set aside.
6. In a medium bowl, combine ricotta, broccoli, Parmesan, 1 cup of mozzarella and remaining 1/2 tsp. salt. Stir until well blended.
7. In a 7x11 inch baking dish layer: 1/4 cup white sauce; 3 noodles; one-third of remaining white sauce; half the broccoli mixture; 3 more noodles; half remaining white sauce; remaining broccoli mixture; 3 noodles; remaining white sauce. Sprinkle with remaining mozzarella. Cover with foil coated with cooking spray.
8. Serve and enjoy!

Broccoli Corn Bread

Ingredients:

2 sm. boxes corn bread mix
1 1/2 sticks butter, melted
1 sm. onion, chopped
5 eggs
2 cup cottage cheese
1 1/2 cups broccoli, chopped

Directions:

1. Preheat oven to 400 degrees F.
2. Mix all ingredients together in a bowl.
3. Pour into large baking dish.
4. Bake for 40 minutes.
5. Serve and enjoy!

Broccoli Bread

Ingredients:

1 cup egg substitute
3/4 cup fat-free cottage cheese
1/2 cup fat-free sour cream
2 tbsps. butter, melted
3/4 tsp. salt
1 1/2 cups finely chopped onion
1 (10-oz.) package frozen chopped broccoli, thawed and drained
1 (8 1/2-oz.) package corn muffin mix
Cooking spray

Directions:

1. Preheat oven to 400 degrees F.
2. Combine first 5 ingredients in a large bowl.
3. Stir in the onion, broccoli, and muffin mix; stir until well blended.
4. Pour into a 13 x 9-inch baking pan coated with cooking spray.
5. Bake for 27 minutes or until set.
6. Serve and enjoy!

Broccoli Squares

Ingredients:

2 (8 oz.) packages refrigerated crescent roll dough
2 (8 oz.) packages cream cheese, softened 1 cup mayonnaise
1 (1 oz.) package dry Ranch-style dressing mix
1 head fresh broccoli, chopped 3 roma (plum) tomatoes, chopped
1 cup shredded Cheddar cheese

Directions:

1. Preheat oven to 375 degrees F (190 degrees C).
2. Lightly grease a medium baking sheet.
3. Arrange the dinner roll dough in 4 rectangles on the baking sheet.
4. Bake in the preheated oven 12 minutes, or until golden brown.
5. Remove from heat and allow to cool completely.
6. In a medium bowl, mix the cream cheese, mayonnaise and dry ranch-style dressing mix. Spread evenly on the crescent rolls. Sprinkle with broccoli and tomatoes.
7. Top with Cheddar cheese and serve.
8. Serve and enjoy!

Broccoli Balls

Ingredients:

1 (10 oz.) package chopped frozen broccoli, thawed
1 (6 oz.) package chicken flavored dry stuffing mix
1/2 cup grated Parmesan cheese 1 medium onion, chopped
6 eggs, beaten
3/4 cup margarine, melted
1 tsp. ground black pepper
1/2 tsp. garlic salt

Directions:

1. Place broccoli in a medium saucepan with enough water to cover. Cover, and bring to a boil. Cook 5 minutes. Uncover, and continue cooking 2 to 3 minutes, until tender. Remove from heat, drain, and cool.
2. In a large bowl, mix broccoli, stuffing mix, Parmesan cheese, onion, eggs, margarine, pepper, and garlic salt. Cover, and chill in the refrigerator approximately 1 hour, until moisture has been absorbed.
3. Preheat oven to 325 degrees F (165 degrees C).
4. Roll the chilled mixture into 1 inch balls, and arrange on a medium baking sheet.
5. Bake 15 to 20 minutes in the preheated oven, until browned.
6. Serve and enjoy!

Broccoli Bites

Ingredients:

2 (10 oz.) packages frozen chopped broccoli 6 eggs
2 tbsps. dried minced onion
1 tsp. dried parsley
1/2 tsp. poultry seasoning
1/2 tsp. salt
1/2 tsp. ground black pepper
1 cup grated Parmesan cheese
2 cups dry bread crumbs
1/2 cup margarine, softened
1/4 cup milk

Directions:

1. Preheat the oven to 350 degrees F (175 degrees C).
2. Cook broccoli according to package directions. Drain, and cool.
3. In a large bowl, whisk together the eggs, onion, parsley, poultry seasoning, salt and pepper. Stir in the bread crumbs, Parmesan cheese, margarine and milk. Mix in the broccoli last.
4. Let the mixture stand for about 10 minutes. It should thicken, but if not, add a little more bread crumbs. Roll the mixture into small balls, and arrange on a greased baking sheet.
5. Bake for 15 to 20 minutes in the preheated oven, until firm and lightly toasted.
6. Serve and enjoy!

Broccoli Nuggets

Ingredients:

1 tsp. vegetable oil, or as needed
1 (16 oz.) package frozen chopped broccoli, thawed
1 cup bread crumbs
1 1/2 cups shredded Cheddar cheese 3 eggs
1/2 tsp. dried basil
1/2 tsp. dried oregano
1/4 tsp. garlic powder

Directions:

1. Preheat oven to 375 degrees F (190 degrees C).
2. Grease a baking sheet with oil.
3. Place a steamer insert into a saucepan and fill with water to just below the bottom of the steamer. Bring water to a boil; add broccoli, cover, and steam until tender, 2 to 6 minutes.
4. Let broccoli cool at room temperature until cool enough to touch.
5. Transfer broccoli into a large mixing bowl. Add bread crumbs, Cheddar cheese, eggs, basil, oregano, and garlic powder to the broccoli; mix. Shape into nuggets or fun shapes and arrange onto the prepared baking sheet.
6. Bake in preheated for 15 minutes, flip, and continue baking until heated through and beginning to firm, 10 to 15 minutes more.
7. Serve and enjoy!

Broccoli Chedder Dip

Ingredients:

1 (16 oz.) container sour cream
1 (10 oz.) package frozen chopped broccoli, thawed and water squeezed out
1 (1 oz.) package ranch dressing mix
1 cup shredded Cheddar cheese, divided

Directions:

1. Preheat oven to 350 degrees F (175 degrees C).
2. Mix sour cream, broccoli, ranch dressing mix, and 3/4 cup Cheddar cheese in a bowl; transfer to an 8x8-inch baking dish.
3. Sprinkle remaining 1/4 cup Cheddar cheese over mixture.
4. Bake in the preheated oven until dip is bubbling and cheese is melted, about 30 minutes.
5. Serve and enjoy!

Broccoli Stuffed Potatoes

Ingredients:

4 large baking potatoes
1 small head broccoli, cut into florets
salt and pepper to taste
3 tbsps. cheese sauce

Directions:

1. Wash potatoes and pierce with a fork. Microwave on high for 15 minutes, or until done.
2. Place broccoli in a steamer over 1 inch of boiling water, and cover. Cook until tender but still firm, about 2 to 6 minutes. Drain.
3. Preheat oven to 350 degrees F (175 degrees C).
4. Slice the tops off of the potatoes, and scoop the flesh into a large bowl with the broccoli.
5. Season with salt and pepper to taste.
6. Stir in cheese sauce and mash mixture until desired consistency is reached, adding more sauce if desired.
7. Spoon mixture back into the skins, and place on a baking sheet.
8. Bake for 30 minutes.
9. Serve and enjoy!

The End

About the Author

Laura Sommers is a loving wife and mother who lives on a small farm in Baltimore County, Maryland and has a passion for all things domestic especially when it comes to saving money. She has a profitable eBay business and is a couponing addict. She challenges herself to write books that are enriching, enjoyable, and often unconventional.

Other books by Laura Sommers

- Easy to Make Party Dip Recipes: Chips and Dips and Salsa and Whips!
- Super Slimming Vegan Soup Recipes!
- Popcorn Lovers Recipe Book
- Inexpensive Low Carb Recipes
- Recipes for the Zombie Apocalypse: Cooking Meals with Shelf Stable Foods
- Best Traditional Irish Recipes for St. Patrick's Day
- Egg Recipes for People With Backyard Chickens
- Awesome Sugar Free Diabetic Pie Recipes
- Super Awesome Traditional Maryland Recipes
- Super Awesome Farm Fresh Pork Chop Recipes

May all of your meals be a banquet
with good friends and good food.

Printed in Great Britain
by Amazon